RECORD LABEL WORKBOOK

SCOTT ORR

Printed in the United States of America.

First Edition, 2021

Published by Other Record Labels.

ISBN 9798724857017

www.otherrecordlabels.com

OTHER RECORD LABELS

GET THE BONUS CONTENT

Visit the back of the book for instructions on how to download **printable versions of this workbook** and to access **additional bonus content.**

Be sure to join our private community of record labels at
http://facebook.otherrecordlabels.com

Get more weekly advice on running a record label at
https://www.otherrecordlabels.com/quick-tips

The Four Pillars of Building a Successful Record Label
Consistency, Persistency, Intentionality, Generosity

*List opportunities you can practice **consistency** with your record label*

_____

_____

_____

_____

_____

_____

_____

_____

*List opportunities you can practice **persistency** with your record label*

_____

_____

_____

_____

_____

_____

_____

_____

_____

The Four Pillars of Building a Successful Record Label
Consistency, Persistency, Intentionality, Generosity

*List opportunities you can practice **intentionality** with your record label*

_____

_____

_____

_____

_____

_____

_____

_____

*List opportunities you can practice **generosity** with your record label*

_____

_____

_____

_____

_____

_____

_____

_____

WHAT MUSIC FORMATS DO THEY PREFER?

HOW DO THEY DISCOVER NEW MUSIC?

WHAT OTHER FORMS OF CULTURE ARE
THEY INTERESTED IN?

WHAT ONLINE COMMUNITIES/PLATFORMS
DO THEY FREQUENT?

OTHER IMPORTANT AUDIENCE DETAILS

NAME CHOICES	SOCIAL AVAILABILITY	URL AVAILABILITY	TRADEMARK CONFLICTS

LOGO CHECKLIST

- ☐ JPG
- ☐ EPS (Vector)
- ☐ Transparent (PNG)
- ☐ Black & White Version
- ☐ Layered Art Files
- ☐ Legibility
- ☐ _____

BRAND CHECKLIST

- ☐ Brand Color(s)
- ☐ Brand Font(s)
- ☐ Logo Usage Guidelines
- ☐ Label Motto/Slogan
- ☐ Brand Preferred Username
- ☐ Socials/URLs Secured
- ☐ _____

LABEL DOCUMENTS CHECKLIST

- ☐ Letterhead
- ☐ Return Address Stickers
- ☐ Invoice Template
- ☐ Receipt Template
- ☐ New Artist Info Sheet
- ☐ Staff Contact List
- ☐ _____

ADDITIONAL BRANDING NOTES

LABEL'S MISSION STATEMENT

LABEL'S OVERALL OBJECTIVE

FINANCIAL OBJECTIVES

CREATIVE OBJECTIVES

SHORT-TERM GOALS

LONG-TERM GOALS

TEAM MEMBER	ROLE	RESPONSIBILITIES

TASKS/RESPONSIBILITIES

MANUFACTURING	MARKETING	DISTRIBUTION

PRESS/PROMO	RADIO/PLAYLISTING	ACCOUNTING/LEGAL

CATALOG ID	ARTIST	TITLE	SKU/BARCODE	RELEASE DATE	FORMATS

HOW TO START A RECORD LABEL   RELEASE SCHEDULE

ARTIST	TITLE	RELEASE DATE

HOW TO START A RECORD LABEL
MONTHLY TO-DO LIST

HOW TO START A RECORD LABEL   TO-DO LIST
MONTH: YEAR:

A&R TASKS

- ☐ ....
- ☐ ....
- ☐ ....
- ☐ ....
- ☐ ....
- ☐ ....
- ☐ ....

MARKETING TASKS

- ☐ ....
- ☐ ....
- ☐ ....
- ☐ ....
- ☐ ....
- ☐ ....
- ☐ ....

ACCOUNTING TASKS

- ☐ ....
- ☐ ....
- ☐ ....
- ☐ ....
- ☐ ....
- ☐ ....
- ☐ ....

BRANDING TASKS

- ☐ ....
- ☐ ....
- ☐ ....
- ☐ ....
- ☐ ....
- ☐ ....
- ☐ ....

LEGAL TASKS

- ☐ ....
- ☐ ....
- ☐ ....
- ☐ ....
- ☐ ....
- ☐ ....
- ☐ ....

DISTRIBUTION TASKS

- ☐ ....
- ☐ ....
- ☐ ....
- ☐ ....
- ☐ ....
- ☐ ....
- ☐ ....

OTHER TASKS

- ☐ ....
- ☐ ....
- ☐ ....
- ☐ ....
- ☐ ....
- ☐ ....
- ☐ ....

GENERAL TASKS

- ☐ ....
- ☐ ....
- ☐ ....
- ☐ ....
- ☐ ....
- ☐ ....
- ☐ ....

HOW TO START A RECORD LABEL   TO-DO LIST
MONTH: YEAR:

A&R TASKS

- [ ]
- [ ]
- [ ]
- [ ]
- [ ]
- [ ]
- [ ]

MARKETING TASKS

- [ ]
- [ ]
- [ ]
- [ ]
- [ ]
- [ ]
- [ ]

ACCOUNTING TASKS

- [ ]
- [ ]
- [ ]
- [ ]
- [ ]
- [ ]
- [ ]

BRANDING TASKS

- [ ]
- [ ]
- [ ]
- [ ]
- [ ]
- [ ]
- [ ]

LEGAL TASKS

- [ ]
- [ ]
- [ ]
- [ ]
- [ ]
- [ ]
- [ ]

DISTRIBUTION TASKS

- [ ]
- [ ]
- [ ]
- [ ]
- [ ]
- [ ]
- [ ]

OTHER TASKS

- [ ]
- [ ]
- [ ]
- [ ]
- [ ]
- [ ]
- [ ]

GENERAL TASKS

- [ ]
- [ ]
- [ ]
- [ ]
- [ ]
- [ ]
- [ ]

HOW TO START A RECORD LABEL   TO-DO LIST
MONTH: YEAR:

A&R TASKS

- [ ] _____
- [ ] _____
- [ ] _____
- [ ] _____
- [ ] _____
- [ ] _____
- [ ] _____

MARKETING TASKS

- [ ] _____
- [ ] _____
- [ ] _____
- [ ] _____
- [ ] _____
- [ ] _____
- [ ] _____

ACCOUNTING TASKS

- [ ] _____
- [ ] _____
- [ ] _____
- [ ] _____
- [ ] _____
- [ ] _____
- [ ] _____

BRANDING TASKS

- [ ] _____
- [ ] _____
- [ ] _____
- [ ] _____
- [ ] _____
- [ ] _____
- [ ] _____

LEGAL TASKS

- [ ] _____
- [ ] _____
- [ ] _____
- [ ] _____
- [ ] _____
- [ ] _____
- [ ] _____

DISTRIBUTION TASKS

- [ ] _____
- [ ] _____
- [ ] _____
- [ ] _____
- [ ] _____
- [ ] _____
- [ ] _____

OTHER TASKS

- [ ] _____
- [ ] _____
- [ ] _____
- [ ] _____
- [ ] _____
- [ ] _____
- [ ] _____

GENERAL TASKS

- [ ] _____
- [ ] _____
- [ ] _____
- [ ] _____
- [ ] _____
- [ ] _____
- [ ] _____

HOW TO START A RECORD LABEL   TO-DO LIST
MONTH: YEAR:

A&R TASKS

- [ ] _____
- [ ] _____
- [ ] _____
- [ ] _____
- [ ] _____
- [ ] _____
- [ ] _____

MARKETING TASKS

- [ ] _____
- [ ] _____
- [ ] _____
- [ ] _____
- [ ] _____
- [ ] _____
- [ ] _____

ACCOUNTING TASKS

- [ ] _____
- [ ] _____
- [ ] _____
- [ ] _____
- [ ] _____
- [ ] _____
- [ ] _____

BRANDING TASKS

- [ ] _____
- [ ] _____
- [ ] _____
- [ ] _____
- [ ] _____
- [ ] _____
- [ ] _____

LEGAL TASKS

- [ ] _____
- [ ] _____
- [ ] _____
- [ ] _____
- [ ] _____
- [ ] _____
- [ ] _____

DISTRIBUTION TASKS

- [ ] _____
- [ ] _____
- [ ] _____
- [ ] _____
- [ ] _____
- [ ] _____
- [ ] _____

OTHER TASKS

- [ ] _____
- [ ] _____
- [ ] _____
- [ ] _____
- [ ] _____
- [ ] _____
- [ ] _____

GENERAL TASKS

- [ ] _____
- [ ] _____
- [ ] _____
- [ ] _____
- [ ] _____
- [ ] _____
- [ ] _____

HOW TO START A RECORD LABEL   TO-DO LIST
MONTH: YEAR:

A&R TASKS

- [ ] ....
- [ ] ....
- [ ] ....
- [ ] ....
- [ ] ....
- [ ] ....
- [ ] ....

MARKETING TASKS

- [ ] ....
- [ ] ....
- [ ] ....
- [ ] ....
- [ ] ....
- [ ] ....
- [ ] ....

ACCOUNTING TASKS

- [ ] ....
- [ ] ....
- [ ] ....
- [ ] ....
- [ ] ....
- [ ] ....
- [ ] ....

BRANDING TASKS

- [ ] ....
- [ ] ....
- [ ] ....
- [ ] ....
- [ ] ....
- [ ] ....
- [ ] ....

LEGAL TASKS

- [ ] ....
- [ ] ....
- [ ] ....
- [ ] ....
- [ ] ....
- [ ] ....
- [ ] ....

DISTRIBUTION TASKS

- [ ] ....
- [ ] ....
- [ ] ....
- [ ] ....
- [ ] ....
- [ ] ....
- [ ] ....

OTHER TASKS

- [ ] ....
- [ ] ....
- [ ] ....
- [ ] ....
- [ ] ....
- [ ] ....
- [ ] ....

GENERAL TASKS

- [ ] ....
- [ ] ....
- [ ] ....
- [ ] ....
- [ ] ....
- [ ] ....
- [ ] ....

HOW TO START A RECORD LABEL   TO-DO LIST
MONTH: YEAR:

A&R TASKS

- [ ]
- [ ]
- [ ]
- [ ]
- [ ]
- [ ]
- [ ]

MARKETING TASKS

- [ ]
- [ ]
- [ ]
- [ ]
- [ ]
- [ ]
- [ ]

ACCOUNTING TASKS

- [ ]
- [ ]
- [ ]
- [ ]
- [ ]
- [ ]
- [ ]

BRANDING TASKS

- [ ]
- [ ]
- [ ]
- [ ]
- [ ]
- [ ]
- [ ]

LEGAL TASKS

- [ ]
- [ ]
- [ ]
- [ ]
- [ ]
- [ ]
- [ ]

DISTRIBUTION TASKS

- [ ]
- [ ]
- [ ]
- [ ]
- [ ]
- [ ]
- [ ]

OTHER TASKS

- [ ]
- [ ]
- [ ]
- [ ]
- [ ]
- [ ]
- [ ]

GENERAL TASKS

- [ ]
- [ ]
- [ ]
- [ ]
- [ ]
- [ ]
- [ ]

HOW TO START A RECORD LABEL   TO-DO LIST
MONTH: YEAR:

A&R TASKS

- ☐ ....
- ☐ ....
- ☐ ....
- ☐ ....
- ☐ ....
- ☐ ....
- ☐ ....

MARKETING TASKS

- ☐ ....
- ☐ ....
- ☐ ....
- ☐ ....
- ☐ ....
- ☐ ....
- ☐ ....

ACCOUNTING TASKS

- ☐ ....
- ☐ ....
- ☐ ....
- ☐ ....
- ☐ ....
- ☐ ....
- ☐ ....

BRANDING TASKS

- ☐ ....
- ☐ ....
- ☐ ....
- ☐ ....
- ☐ ....
- ☐ ....
- ☐ ....

LEGAL TASKS

- ☐ ....
- ☐ ....
- ☐ ....
- ☐ ....
- ☐ ....
- ☐ ....
- ☐ ....

DISTRIBUTION TASKS

- ☐ ....
- ☐ ....
- ☐ ....
- ☐ ....
- ☐ ....
- ☐ ....
- ☐ ....

OTHER TASKS

- ☐ ....
- ☐ ....
- ☐ ....
- ☐ ....
- ☐ ....
- ☐ ....
- ☐ ....

GENERAL TASKS

- ☐ ....
- ☐ ....
- ☐ ....
- ☐ ....
- ☐ ....
- ☐ ....
- ☐ ....

HOW TO START A RECORD LABEL TO-DO LIST
MONTH: YEAR:

A&R TASKS

- [ ]
- [ ]
- [ ]
- [ ]
- [ ]
- [ ]
- [ ]

MARKETING TASKS

- [ ]
- [ ]
- [ ]
- [ ]
- [ ]
- [ ]
- [ ]

ACCOUNTING TASKS

- [ ]
- [ ]
- [ ]
- [ ]
- [ ]
- [ ]
- [ ]

BRANDING TASKS

- [ ]
- [ ]
- [ ]
- [ ]
- [ ]
- [ ]
- [ ]

LEGAL TASKS

- [ ]
- [ ]
- [ ]
- [ ]
- [ ]
- [ ]
- [ ]

DISTRIBUTION TASKS

- [ ]
- [ ]
- [ ]
- [ ]
- [ ]
- [ ]
- [ ]

OTHER TASKS

- [ ]
- [ ]
- [ ]
- [ ]
- [ ]
- [ ]
- [ ]

GENERAL TASKS

- [ ]
- [ ]
- [ ]
- [ ]
- [ ]
- [ ]
- [ ]

HOW TO START A RECORD LABEL   TO-DO LIST
MONTH: YEAR:

A&R TASKS

- [ ] _____
- [ ] _____
- [ ] _____
- [ ] _____
- [ ] _____
- [ ] _____
- [ ] _____

MARKETING TASKS

- [ ] _____
- [ ] _____
- [ ] _____
- [ ] _____
- [ ] _____
- [ ] _____
- [ ] _____

ACCOUNTING TASKS

- [ ] _____
- [ ] _____
- [ ] _____
- [ ] _____
- [ ] _____
- [ ] _____
- [ ] _____

BRANDING TASKS

- [ ] _____
- [ ] _____
- [ ] _____
- [ ] _____
- [ ] _____
- [ ] _____
- [ ] _____

LEGAL TASKS

- [ ] _____
- [ ] _____
- [ ] _____
- [ ] _____
- [ ] _____
- [ ] _____
- [ ] _____

DISTRIBUTION TASKS

- [ ] _____
- [ ] _____
- [ ] _____
- [ ] _____
- [ ] _____
- [ ] _____
- [ ] _____

OTHER TASKS

- [ ] _____
- [ ] _____
- [ ] _____
- [ ] _____
- [ ] _____
- [ ] _____
- [ ] _____

GENERAL TASKS

- [ ] _____
- [ ] _____
- [ ] _____
- [ ] _____
- [ ] _____
- [ ] _____
- [ ] _____

HOW TO START A RECORD LABEL   TO-DO LIST
MONTH: YEAR:

A&R TASKS

- [ ]
- [ ]
- [ ]
- [ ]
- [ ]
- [ ]
- [ ]

MARKETING TASKS

- [ ]
- [ ]
- [ ]
- [ ]
- [ ]
- [ ]
- [ ]

ACCOUNTING TASKS

- [ ]
- [ ]
- [ ]
- [ ]
- [ ]
- [ ]
- [ ]

BRANDING TASKS

- [ ]
- [ ]
- [ ]
- [ ]
- [ ]
- [ ]
- [ ]

LEGAL TASKS

- [ ]
- [ ]
- [ ]
- [ ]
- [ ]
- [ ]
- [ ]

DISTRIBUTION TASKS

- [ ]
- [ ]
- [ ]
- [ ]
- [ ]
- [ ]
- [ ]

OTHER TASKS

- [ ]
- [ ]
- [ ]
- [ ]
- [ ]
- [ ]
- [ ]

GENERAL TASKS

- [ ]
- [ ]
- [ ]
- [ ]
- [ ]
- [ ]
- [ ]

HOW TO START A RECORD LABEL   TO-DO LIST
MONTH: YEAR:

A&R TASKS
- [ ] ....
- [ ] ....
- [ ] ....
- [ ] ....
- [ ] ....
- [ ] ....
- [ ] ....

MARKETING TASKS
- [ ] ....
- [ ] ....
- [ ] ....
- [ ] ....
- [ ] ....
- [ ] ....
- [ ] ....

ACCOUNTING TASKS
- [ ] ....
- [ ] ....
- [ ] ....
- [ ] ....
- [ ] ....
- [ ] ....
- [ ] ....

BRANDING TASKS
- [ ] ....
- [ ] ....
- [ ] ....
- [ ] ....
- [ ] ....
- [ ] ....
- [ ] ....

LEGAL TASKS
- [ ] ....
- [ ] ....
- [ ] ....
- [ ] ....
- [ ] ....
- [ ] ....
- [ ] ....

DISTRIBUTION TASKS
- [ ] ....
- [ ] ....
- [ ] ....
- [ ] ....
- [ ] ....
- [ ] ....
- [ ] ....

OTHER TASKS
- [ ] ....
- [ ] ....
- [ ] ....
- [ ] ....
- [ ] ....
- [ ] ....
- [ ] ....

GENERAL TASKS
- [ ] ....
- [ ] ....
- [ ] ....
- [ ] ....
- [ ] ....
- [ ] ....
- [ ] ....

HOW TO START A RECORD LABEL   TO-DO LIST
MONTH: YEAR:

A&R TASKS

- [ ] _____
- [ ] _____
- [ ] _____
- [ ] _____
- [ ] _____
- [ ] _____
- [ ] _____

MARKETING TASKS

- [ ] _____
- [ ] _____
- [ ] _____
- [ ] _____
- [ ] _____
- [ ] _____
- [ ] _____

ACCOUNTING TASKS

- [ ] _____
- [ ] _____
- [ ] _____
- [ ] _____
- [ ] _____
- [ ] _____
- [ ] _____

BRANDING TASKS

- [ ] _____
- [ ] _____
- [ ] _____
- [ ] _____
- [ ] _____
- [ ] _____
- [ ] _____

LEGAL TASKS

- [ ] _____
- [ ] _____
- [ ] _____
- [ ] _____
- [ ] _____
- [ ] _____
- [ ] _____

DISTRIBUTION TASKS

- [ ] _____
- [ ] _____
- [ ] _____
- [ ] _____
- [ ] _____
- [ ] _____
- [ ] _____

OTHER TASKS

- [ ] _____
- [ ] _____
- [ ] _____
- [ ] _____
- [ ] _____
- [ ] _____
- [ ] _____

GENERAL TASKS

- [ ] _____
- [ ] _____
- [ ] _____
- [ ] _____
- [ ] _____
- [ ] _____
- [ ] _____

Visit **otherrecordlabels.com/workbook** to download a printable versions of these pages!

HOW TO START A RECORD LABEL   CONTACT LIST

PUBLICATION/COMPANY	NAME	CONTACT INFO	NOTES

HOW TO START A RECORD LABEL   CONTACT LIST

PUBLICATION/COMPANY	NAME	CONTACT INFO	NOTES

LEVEL 3 GOALS   (WHAT YOU REALLY WANT TO DO)

LEVEL 2 GOALS   (WHAT YOU THINK YOU CAN DO)

LEVEL 1 GOALS   (WHAT YOU KNOW YOU CAN DO)

YEAR AT A GLANCE

YEAR:

LEVEL 3 GOALS   (WHAT YOU REALLY WANT TO DO)

LEVEL 2 GOALS   (WHAT YOU THINK YOU CAN DO)

LEVEL 1 GOALS   (WHAT YOU KNOW YOU CAN DO)

HOW TO START A RECORD LABEL   WEEK AT A GLANCE

Visit **otherrecordlabels.com/workbook** to download a printable versions of these pages!

WEEK AT A GLANCE

WEEK OF _____ / _____ / 20 _____

HIGH PRIORITY TASKS

☐ ☐ ☐ ☐ ☐ ☐ ☐

MEDIUM PRIORITY TASKS

☐ ☐ ☐ ☐ ☐ ☐

ADDITIONAL TASKS

☐ ☐ ☐ ☐

NOTES

PRODUCTIVITY SCORE   1   2   3   4   5   6   7   8   9   10

WEEK AT A GLANCE

WEEK OF _____ / _____ / 20 _____

HIGH PRIORITY TASKS

☐ ☐ ☐ ☐ ☐ ☐ ☐

MEDIUM PRIORITY TASKS

☐ ☐ ☐ ☐ ☐ ☐

ADDITIONAL TASKS

☐ ☐ ☐ ☐

NOTES

PRODUCTIVITY SCORE   1   2   3   4   5   6   7   8   9   10

WEEK AT A GLANCE

WEEK OF _____ / _____ / 20 _____

HIGH PRIORITY TASKS

☐
☐
☐
☐
☐
☐
☐

MEDIUM PRIORITY TASKS

☐
☐
☐
☐
☐
☐

ADDITIONAL TASKS

☐
☐
☐
☐

NOTES

PRODUCTIVITY SCORE   1   2   3   4   5   6   7   8   9   10

WEEK AT A GLANCE

WEEK OF _____ / _____ / 20 _____

HIGH PRIORITY TASKS

☐
☐
☐
☐
☐
☐
☐

MEDIUM PRIORITY TASKS

☐
☐
☐
☐
☐
☐

ADDITIONAL TASKS

☐
☐
☐
☐

NOTES

PRODUCTIVITY SCORE   1   2   3   4   5   6   7   8   9   10

WEEK AT A GLANCE

WEEK OF _____ / _____ / 20 _____

HIGH PRIORITY TASKS

☐ ☐ ☐ ☐ ☐ ☐ ☐

MEDIUM PRIORITY TASKS

☐ ☐ ☐ ☐ ☐ ☐

ADDITIONAL TASKS

☐ ☐ ☐ ☐

NOTES

PRODUCTIVITY SCORE 1 2 3 4 5 6 7 8 9 10

WEEK AT A GLANCE

WEEK OF _____ / _____ / 20 _____

HIGH PRIORITY TASKS

☐ ☐ ☐ ☐ ☐ ☐ ☐

MEDIUM PRIORITY TASKS

☐ ☐ ☐ ☐ ☐ ☐

ADDITIONAL TASKS

☐ ☐ ☐ ☐

NOTES

PRODUCTIVITY SCORE 1 2 3 4 5 6 7 8 9 10

WEEK AT A GLANCE

WEEK OF _____ / _____ / 20 _____

HIGH PRIORITY TASKS

☐ ☐ ☐ ☐ ☐ ☐ ☐

MEDIUM PRIORITY TASKS

☐ ☐ ☐ ☐ ☐ ☐

ADDITIONAL TASKS

☐ ☐ ☐ ☐

NOTES

PRODUCTIVITY SCORE   1   2   3   4   5   6   7   8   9   10

WEEK AT A GLANCE

WEEK OF _____ / _____ / 20 _____

HIGH PRIORITY TASKS

☐ ☐ ☐ ☐ ☐ ☐ ☐

MEDIUM PRIORITY TASKS

☐ ☐ ☐ ☐ ☐ ☐

ADDITIONAL TASKS

☐ ☐ ☐ ☐

NOTES

PRODUCTIVITY SCORE   1   2   3   4   5   6   7   8   9   10

WEEK AT A GLANCE

WEEK OF _____ / _____ / 20 _____

HIGH PRIORITY TASKS

☐ ☐ ☐ ☐ ☐ ☐ ☐

MEDIUM PRIORITY TASKS

☐ ☐ ☐ ☐ ☐ ☐

ADDITIONAL TASKS

☐ ☐ ☐ ☐

NOTES

PRODUCTIVITY SCORE   1   2   3   4   5   6   7   8   9   10

WEEK AT A GLANCE

WEEK OF _____ / _____ / 20 _____

HIGH PRIORITY TASKS

☐ ☐ ☐ ☐ ☐ ☐ ☐

MEDIUM PRIORITY TASKS

☐ ☐ ☐ ☐ ☐ ☐

ADDITIONAL TASKS

☐ ☐ ☐ ☐

NOTES

PRODUCTIVITY SCORE   1   2   3   4   5   6   7   8   9   10

WEEK AT A GLANCE

WEEK OF _____ / _____ / 20 _____

HIGH PRIORITY TASKS

MEDIUM PRIORITY TASKS

ADDITIONAL TASKS

NOTES

PRODUCTIVITY SCORE 1 2 3 4 5 6 7 8 9 10

WEEK AT A GLANCE

WEEK OF _____ / _____ / 20 _____

HIGH PRIORITY TASKS

MEDIUM PRIORITY TASKS

ADDITIONAL TASKS

NOTES

PRODUCTIVITY SCORE 1 2 3 4 5 6 7 8 9 10

WEEK AT A GLANCE

HIGH PRIORITY TASKS

☐ ☐ ☐ ☐ ☐ ☐ ☐

MEDIUM PRIORITY TASKS

☐ ☐ ☐ ☐ ☐ ☐

ADDITIONAL TASKS

☐ ☐ ☐ ☐

NOTES

PRODUCTIVITY SCORE   1   2   3   4   5   6   7   8   9   10

WEEK AT A GLANCE

HIGH PRIORITY TASKS

☐ ☐ ☐ ☐ ☐ ☐ ☐

MEDIUM PRIORITY TASKS

☐ ☐ ☐ ☐ ☐ ☐

ADDITIONAL TASKS

☐ ☐ ☐ ☐

NOTES

PRODUCTIVITY SCORE   1   2   3   4   5   6   7   8   9   10

WEEK AT A GLANCE

WEEK OF _____ / _____ / 20 _____

HIGH PRIORITY TASKS

☐
☐
☐
☐
☐
☐
☐

MEDIUM PRIORITY TASKS

☐
☐
☐
☐
☐
☐

ADDITIONAL TASKS

☐
☐
☐
☐

NOTES

PRODUCTIVITY SCORE   1   2   3   4   5   6   7   8   9   10

WEEK AT A GLANCE

WEEK OF _____ / _____ / 20 _____

HIGH PRIORITY TASKS

☐
☐
☐
☐
☐
☐
☐

MEDIUM PRIORITY TASKS

☐
☐
☐
☐
☐
☐

ADDITIONAL TASKS

☐
☐
☐
☐

NOTES

PRODUCTIVITY SCORE   1   2   3   4   5   6   7   8   9   10

WEEK AT A GLANCE

WEEK OF _____ / _____ / 20 _____

HIGH PRIORITY TASKS

☐ ☐ ☐ ☐ ☐ ☐ ☐

MEDIUM PRIORITY TASKS

☐ ☐ ☐ ☐ ☐ ☐

ADDITIONAL TASKS

☐ ☐ ☐ ☐

NOTES

PRODUCTIVITY SCORE   1   2   3   4   5   6   7   8   9   10

WEEK AT A GLANCE

WEEK OF _____ / _____ / 20 _____

HIGH PRIORITY TASKS

☐ ☐ ☐ ☐ ☐ ☐ ☐

MEDIUM PRIORITY TASKS

☐ ☐ ☐ ☐ ☐ ☐

ADDITIONAL TASKS

☐ ☐ ☐ ☐

NOTES

PRODUCTIVITY SCORE   1   2   3   4   5   6   7   8   9   10

46

WEEK AT A GLANCE

WEEK OF _____ / _____ / 20 _____

HIGH PRIORITY TASKS

☐ ☐ ☐ ☐ ☐ ☐ ☐

MEDIUM PRIORITY TASKS

☐ ☐ ☐ ☐ ☐ ☐

ADDITIONAL TASKS

☐ ☐ ☐ ☐

NOTES

PRODUCTIVITY SCORE 1 2 3 4 5 6 7 8 9 10

WEEK AT A GLANCE

WEEK OF _____ / _____ / 20 _____

HIGH PRIORITY TASKS

☐ ☐ ☐ ☐ ☐ ☐ ☐

MEDIUM PRIORITY TASKS

☐ ☐ ☐ ☐ ☐ ☐

ADDITIONAL TASKS

☐ ☐ ☐ ☐

NOTES

PRODUCTIVITY SCORE 1 2 3 4 5 6 7 8 9 10

WEEK AT A GLANCE

WEEK OF _____ / _____ / 20 _____

HIGH PRIORITY TASKS

☐ ☐ ☐ ☐ ☐ ☐ ☐

MEDIUM PRIORITY TASKS

☐ ☐ ☐ ☐ ☐ ☐

ADDITIONAL TASKS

☐ ☐ ☐ ☐

NOTES

PRODUCTIVITY SCORE   1   2   3   4   5   6   7   8   9   10

WEEK AT A GLANCE

WEEK OF _____ / _____ / 20 _____

HIGH PRIORITY TASKS

☐ ☐ ☐ ☐ ☐ ☐ ☐

MEDIUM PRIORITY TASKS

☐ ☐ ☐ ☐ ☐ ☐

ADDITIONAL TASKS

☐ ☐ ☐ ☐

NOTES

PRODUCTIVITY SCORE   1   2   3   4   5   6   7   8   9   10

WEEK AT A GLANCE

WEEK OF _____ / _____ / 20 _____

HIGH PRIORITY TASKS

☐ ☐ ☐ ☐ ☐ ☐ ☐

MEDIUM PRIORITY TASKS

☐ ☐ ☐ ☐ ☐ ☐

ADDITIONAL TASKS

☐ ☐ ☐ ☐

NOTES

PRODUCTIVITY SCORE 1 2 3 4 5 6 7 8 9 10

WEEK AT A GLANCE

WEEK OF _____ / _____ / 20 _____

HIGH PRIORITY TASKS

☐ ☐ ☐ ☐ ☐ ☐ ☐

MEDIUM PRIORITY TASKS

☐ ☐ ☐ ☐ ☐ ☐

ADDITIONAL TASKS

☐ ☐ ☐ ☐

NOTES

PRODUCTIVITY SCORE 1 2 3 4 5 6 7 8 9 10

WEEK AT A GLANCE

HIGH PRIORITY TASKS

☐ ☐ ☐ ☐ ☐ ☐ ☐

MEDIUM PRIORITY TASKS

☐ ☐ ☐ ☐ ☐ ☐

ADDITIONAL TASKS

☐ ☐ ☐ ☐

NOTES

PRODUCTIVITY SCORE   1   2   3   4   5   6   7   8   9   10

WEEK AT A GLANCE

WEEK OF _____ / _____ / 20 _____

HIGH PRIORITY TASKS

☐ ☐ ☐ ☐ ☐ ☐ ☐

MEDIUM PRIORITY TASKS

☐ ☐ ☐ ☐ ☐ ☐

ADDITIONAL TASKS

☐ ☐ ☐ ☐

NOTES

PRODUCTIVITY SCORE   1   2   3   4   5   6   7   8   9   10

WEEK AT A GLANCE

WEEK OF _____ / _____ / 20 _____

HIGH PRIORITY TASKS

MEDIUM PRIORITY TASKS

ADDITIONAL TASKS

NOTES

PRODUCTIVITY SCORE 1 2 3 4 5 6 7 8 9 10

WEEK AT A GLANCE

WEEK OF _____ / _____ / 20 _____

HIGH PRIORITY TASKS

MEDIUM PRIORITY TASKS

ADDITIONAL TASKS

NOTES

PRODUCTIVITY SCORE 1 2 3 4 5 6 7 8 9 10

WEEK AT A GLANCE

WEEK OF _____ / _____ / 20 _____

HIGH PRIORITY TASKS

☐ ☐ ☐ ☐ ☐ ☐ ☐

MEDIUM PRIORITY TASKS

☐ ☐ ☐ ☐ ☐ ☐

ADDITIONAL TASKS

☐ ☐ ☐ ☐

NOTES

PRODUCTIVITY SCORE

1 2 3 4 5 6 7 8 9 10

WEEK AT A GLANCE

WEEK OF _____ / _____ / 20 _____

HIGH PRIORITY TASKS

☐ ☐ ☐ ☐ ☐ ☐ ☐

MEDIUM PRIORITY TASKS

☐ ☐ ☐ ☐ ☐ ☐

ADDITIONAL TASKS

☐ ☐ ☐ ☐

NOTES

PRODUCTIVITY SCORE

1 2 3 4 5 6 7 8 9 10

WEEK AT A GLANCE

WEEK OF _____ / _____ / 20_____

HIGH PRIORITY TASKS

☐ ☐ ☐ ☐ ☐ ☐ ☐

MEDIUM PRIORITY TASKS

☐ ☐ ☐ ☐ ☐ ☐

ADDITIONAL TASKS

☐ ☐ ☐ ☐

NOTES

PRODUCTIVITY SCORE 1 2 3 4 5 6 7 8 9 10

WEEK AT A GLANCE

WEEK OF _____ / _____ / 20_____

HIGH PRIORITY TASKS

☐ ☐ ☐ ☐ ☐ ☐ ☐

MEDIUM PRIORITY TASKS

☐ ☐ ☐ ☐ ☐ ☐

ADDITIONAL TASKS

☐ ☐ ☐ ☐

NOTES

PRODUCTIVITY SCORE 1 2 3 4 5 6 7 8 9 10

WEEK AT A GLANCE

WEEK OF _____ / _____ / 20 _____

HIGH PRIORITY TASKS

MEDIUM PRIORITY TASKS

ADDITIONAL TASKS

NOTES

PRODUCTIVITY SCORE   1   2   3   4   5   6   7   8   9   10

WEEK AT A GLANCE

WEEK OF _____ / _____ / 20 _____

HIGH PRIORITY TASKS

MEDIUM PRIORITY TASKS

ADDITIONAL TASKS

NOTES

PRODUCTIVITY SCORE   1   2   3   4   5   6   7   8   9   10

WEEK AT A GLANCE

WEEK OF _____ / _____ / 20_____

HIGH PRIORITY TASKS

☐ ☐ ☐ ☐ ☐ ☐ ☐

MEDIUM PRIORITY TASKS

☐ ☐ ☐ ☐ ☐ ☐

ADDITIONAL TASKS

☐ ☐ ☐ ☐

NOTES

PRODUCTIVITY SCORE 1 2 3 4 5 6 7 8 9 10

WEEK AT A GLANCE

WEEK OF _____ / _____ / 20_____

HIGH PRIORITY TASKS

☐ ☐ ☐ ☐ ☐ ☐ ☐

MEDIUM PRIORITY TASKS

☐ ☐ ☐ ☐ ☐ ☐

ADDITIONAL TASKS

☐ ☐ ☐ ☐

NOTES

PRODUCTIVITY SCORE 1 2 3 4 5 6 7 8 9 10

WEEK OF _____ / _____ / 20 _____

HIGH PRIORITY TASKS

☐ ☐ ☐ ☐ ☐ ☐ ☐

MEDIUM PRIORITY TASKS

☐ ☐ ☐ ☐ ☐ ☐

ADDITIONAL TASKS

☐ ☐ ☐ ☐

NOTES

PRODUCTIVITY SCORE   1   2   3   4   5   6   7   8   9   10

WEEK AT A GLANCE

WEEK OF _____ / _____ / 20 _____

HIGH PRIORITY TASKS

☐ ☐ ☐ ☐ ☐ ☐ ☐

MEDIUM PRIORITY TASKS

☐ ☐ ☐ ☐ ☐ ☐

ADDITIONAL TASKS

☐ ☐ ☐ ☐

NOTES

PRODUCTIVITY SCORE   1   2   3   4   5   6   7   8   9   10

WEEK AT A GLANCE

WEEK OF _____ / _____ / 20 _____

HIGH PRIORITY TASKS

☐ ☐ ☐ ☐ ☐ ☐ ☐

MEDIUM PRIORITY TASKS

☐ ☐ ☐ ☐ ☐ ☐

ADDITIONAL TASKS

☐ ☐ ☐ ☐

NOTES

PRODUCTIVITY SCORE   1   2   3   4   5   6   7   8   9   10

WEEK AT A GLANCE

WEEK OF _____ / _____ / 20 _____

HIGH PRIORITY TASKS

☐ ☐ ☐ ☐ ☐ ☐ ☐

MEDIUM PRIORITY TASKS

☐ ☐ ☐ ☐ ☐ ☐

ADDITIONAL TASKS

☐ ☐ ☐ ☐

NOTES

PRODUCTIVITY SCORE   1   2   3   4   5   6   7   8   9   10

WEEK AT A GLANCE

WEEK OF _____ / _____ / 20 _____

HIGH PRIORITY TASKS

☐ ☐ ☐ ☐ ☐ ☐ ☐

MEDIUM PRIORITY TASKS

☐ ☐ ☐ ☐ ☐ ☐

ADDITIONAL TASKS

☐ ☐ ☐ ☐

NOTES

PRODUCTIVITY SCORE   1   2   3   4   5   6   7   8   9   10

WEEK AT A GLANCE

WEEK OF _____ / _____ / 20 _____

HIGH PRIORITY TASKS

☐ ☐ ☐ ☐ ☐ ☐ ☐

MEDIUM PRIORITY TASKS

☐ ☐ ☐ ☐ ☐ ☐

ADDITIONAL TASKS

☐ ☐ ☐ ☐

NOTES

PRODUCTIVITY SCORE   1   2   3   4   5   6   7   8   9   10

WEEK AT A GLANCE

WEEK OF _____ / _____ / 20_____

HIGH PRIORITY TASKS

☐ ☐ ☐ ☐ ☐ ☐ ☐

MEDIUM PRIORITY TASKS

☐ ☐ ☐ ☐ ☐ ☐

ADDITIONAL TASKS

☐ ☐ ☐ ☐

NOTES

PRODUCTIVITY SCORE   1   2   3   4   5   6   7   8   9   10

WEEK AT A GLANCE

WEEK OF _____ / _____ / 20_____

HIGH PRIORITY TASKS

☐ ☐ ☐ ☐ ☐ ☐ ☐

MEDIUM PRIORITY TASKS

☐ ☐ ☐ ☐ ☐ ☐

ADDITIONAL TASKS

☐ ☐ ☐ ☐

NOTES

PRODUCTIVITY SCORE   1   2   3   4   5   6   7   8   9   10

WEEK AT A GLANCE

WEEK OF _____ / _____ / 20 _____

HIGH PRIORITY TASKS

☐ ☐ ☐ ☐ ☐ ☐ ☐

MEDIUM PRIORITY TASKS

☐ ☐ ☐ ☐ ☐ ☐

ADDITIONAL TASKS

☐ ☐ ☐ ☐

NOTES

PRODUCTIVITY SCORE   1   2   3   4   5   6   7   8   9   10

WEEK AT A GLANCE

WEEK OF _____ / _____ / 20 _____

HIGH PRIORITY TASKS

☐ ☐ ☐ ☐ ☐ ☐ ☐

MEDIUM PRIORITY TASKS

☐ ☐ ☐ ☐ ☐ ☐

ADDITIONAL TASKS

☐ ☐ ☐ ☐

NOTES

PRODUCTIVITY SCORE   1   2   3   4   5   6   7   8   9   10

WEEK AT A GLANCE

WEEK OF _____ / _____ / 20_____

HIGH PRIORITY TASKS

MEDIUM PRIORITY TASKS

ADDITIONAL TASKS

NOTES

PRODUCTIVITY SCORE   1   2   3   4   5   6   7   8   9   10

WEEK AT A GLANCE

WEEK OF _____ / _____ / 20_____

HIGH PRIORITY TASKS

MEDIUM PRIORITY TASKS

ADDITIONAL TASKS

NOTES

PRODUCTIVITY SCORE   1   2   3   4   5   6   7   8   9   10

WEEK AT A GLANCE

WEEK OF _____ / _____ / 20 _____

HIGH PRIORITY TASKS

☐ ☐ ☐ ☐ ☐ ☐ ☐

MEDIUM PRIORITY TASKS

☐ ☐ ☐ ☐ ☐ ☐

ADDITIONAL TASKS

☐ ☐ ☐ ☐

NOTES

PRODUCTIVITY SCORE   1   2   3   4   5   6   7   8   9   10

WEEK AT A GLANCE

WEEK OF _____ / _____ / 20 _____

HIGH PRIORITY TASKS

☐ ☐ ☐ ☐ ☐ ☐ ☐

MEDIUM PRIORITY TASKS

☐ ☐ ☐ ☐ ☐ ☐

ADDITIONAL TASKS

☐ ☐ ☐ ☐

NOTES

PRODUCTIVITY SCORE   1   2   3   4   5   6   7   8   9   10

WEEK AT A GLANCE

WEEK OF _____ / _____ / 20_____

HIGH PRIORITY TASKS

☐ ☐ ☐ ☐ ☐ ☐ ☐

MEDIUM PRIORITY TASKS

☐ ☐ ☐ ☐ ☐ ☐

ADDITIONAL TASKS

☐ ☐ ☐ ☐

NOTES

PRODUCTIVITY SCORE

1 2 3 4 5 6 7 8 9 10

WEEK AT A GLANCE

WEEK OF _____ / _____ / 20_____

HIGH PRIORITY TASKS

☐ ☐ ☐ ☐ ☐ ☐ ☐

MEDIUM PRIORITY TASKS

☐ ☐ ☐ ☐ ☐ ☐

ADDITIONAL TASKS

☐ ☐ ☐ ☐

NOTES

PRODUCTIVITY SCORE

1 2 3 4 5 6 7 8 9 10

HOW TO START A RECORD LABEL   MONTH AT A GLANCE

Visit **otherrecordlabels.com/workbook** to download a printable versions of these pages!

JANUARY AT A GLANCE

YEAR:

LEVEL 3 GOALS   (WHAT YOU REALLY WANT TO DO)

....

....

....

LEVEL 2 GOALS   (WHAT YOU THINK YOU CAN DO)

....

....

....

....

LEVEL 1 GOALS   (WHAT YOU KNOW YOU CAN DO)

....

....

....

....

....

FEBRUARY AT A GLANCE

LEVEL 3 GOALS   (WHAT YOU REALLY WANT TO DO)

LEVEL 2 GOALS   (WHAT YOU THINK YOU CAN DO)

LEVEL 1 GOALS   (WHAT YOU KNOW YOU CAN DO)

MARCH AT A GLANCE

YEAR:

LEVEL 3 GOALS   (WHAT YOU REALLY WANT TO DO)

_____

_____

_____

LEVEL 2 GOALS   (WHAT YOU THINK YOU CAN DO)

_____

_____

_____

LEVEL 1 GOALS   (WHAT YOU KNOW YOU CAN DO)

_____

_____

_____

_____

APRIL AT A GLANCE

YEAR:

LEVEL 3 GOALS   (WHAT YOU REALLY WANT TO DO)

LEVEL 2 GOALS   (WHAT YOU THINK YOU CAN DO)

LEVEL 1 GOALS   (WHAT YOU KNOW YOU CAN DO)

LEVEL 3 GOALS   (WHAT YOU REALLY WANT TO DO)

LEVEL 2 GOALS   (WHAT YOU THINK YOU CAN DO)

LEVEL 1 GOALS   (WHAT YOU KNOW YOU CAN DO)

JUNE AT A GLANCE

YEAR:

LEVEL 3 GOALS   (WHAT YOU REALLY WANT TO DO)

LEVEL 2 GOALS   (WHAT YOU THINK YOU CAN DO)

LEVEL 1 GOALS   (WHAT YOU KNOW YOU CAN DO)

JULY AT A GLANCE

YEAR:

LEVEL 3 GOALS   (WHAT YOU REALLY WANT TO DO)

LEVEL 2 GOALS   (WHAT YOU THINK YOU CAN DO)

LEVEL 1 GOALS   (WHAT YOU KNOW YOU CAN DO)

YEAR:

LEVEL 3 GOALS   (WHAT YOU REALLY WANT TO DO)

LEVEL 2 GOALS   (WHAT YOU THINK YOU CAN DO)

LEVEL 1 GOALS   (WHAT YOU KNOW YOU CAN DO)

LEVEL 3 GOALS   (WHAT YOU REALLY WANT TO DO)

....

....

....

LEVEL 2 GOALS   (WHAT YOU THINK YOU CAN DO)

....

....

....

LEVEL 1 GOALS   (WHAT YOU KNOW YOU CAN DO)

....

....

....

....

OCTOBER AT A GLANCE

YEAR:

LEVEL 3 GOALS (WHAT YOU REALLY WANT TO DO)

LEVEL 2 GOALS (WHAT YOU THINK YOU CAN DO)

LEVEL 1 GOALS (WHAT YOU KNOW YOU CAN DO)

YEAR:

LEVEL 3 GOALS   (WHAT YOU REALLY WANT TO DO)

LEVEL 2 GOALS   (WHAT YOU THINK YOU CAN DO)

LEVEL 1 GOALS   (WHAT YOU KNOW YOU CAN DO)

LEVEL 3 GOALS   (WHAT YOU REALLY WANT TO DO)

_____

_____

_____

LEVEL 2 GOALS   (WHAT YOU THINK YOU CAN DO)

_____

_____

_____

LEVEL 1 GOALS   (WHAT YOU KNOW YOU CAN DO)

_____

_____

_____

_____

HOW TO START A RECORD LABEL   CHECKLIST

1. Pick a Name
- ☐ Make it unique and easy to search
- ☐ Check social media availability
- ☐ Watch out for copyright infringement

2. Create a Mission Statement
- ☐ What are your values?
- ☐ What are your goals for the label?
- ☐ What is your "why"?

3. Define Your Audience
- ☐ Who is your customer?
- ☐ What does your community/niche look like?
- ☐ What elements of music excite them?

4. Create Your Brand
- ☐ Make a logo (jpg, eps, png)
- ☐ Create brand guidelines to help you look consistent
- ☐ Create banners/profile pictures for social media platforms

5. Secure Social Media Accounts
- ☐ Register and hold as a placeholder
- ☐ Use the same account name for every social platform
- ☐ Use consistent branding for banners and icons

6. Make a Website
- ☐ Don't overthink it
- ☐ Keep it simple and sustainable
- ☐ Don't have a blog or news section that is hard to keep updated
- ☐ Make sure it has links to
    - I. Social Media, Bandcamp, Artist's Pages, Label Playlist (Spotify)
- ☐ Use solely your label Bandcamp page if necessary

7. Keep it Secret
- ☐ Recognize your "entrepreneurial seizure" and temper your excitement
- ☐ Work out the kinks before you go public
- ☐ Shock your audience with something fully fleshed out

8. Create a Label Sampler
- ☐ Ongoing Spotify playlist
- ☐ Bandcamp sampler for free download
- ☐ CD, vinyl, or cassette sampler

9. Find a "Test Artist"
- ☐ Self-release your own music or band first
- ☐ Make sure you outline each others' expectations
- ☐ Be transparent and vulnerable with your first signing

10. Do You Need a Contract?
- ☐ A legal agreement vs. handshake agreement
- ☐ Talk openly with the artist well beforehand
- ☐ Use and save an email thread outlining your agreements
- ☐ Consult a lawyer

11. Establish Expectations
- ☐ Things you won't do as a label
    - II. Things that aren't normally a label's responsibility
    - III. Things that are against your mission statement
- ☐ Things you can't do as a label
    - I. Things you aren't good at
- ☐ Things you hope to do

12. Managing Royalties
- ☐ Plan when to pay your artists
    - I. Monthly, Bi-Monthly, Quarterly
- ☐ What percentage should you pay them? 50%, 60%, 70%?
- ☐ Make sure you remember to deduct expenses
- ☐ Keep an online, ongoing shared document with the artists

13. Managing a Budget
- ☐ Keep track of things using accounting software or Google Sheets
- ☐ Offence vs. Defense
    - I. Making money is like playing offense
    - II. Keeping your expenses down is like playing defense
- ☐ Keep your receipts for everything
- ☐ Make things open and transparent at all times

14. Plan Your Launch
- ☐ Pick a day to launch your label
- ☐ Don't launch any music yet, give your label it's day in the sun
- ☐ Launch (social media, website, logo) all at one
- ☐ Reach out to press prior to launch to announce your label
- ☐ Identify your unique offering to the music world
    - I. Geographic uniqueness
    - II. Sound/aesthetic uniqueness
    - III. Values/mission uniqueness

15. Build an Email List

- ☐ Giveaway something in exchange for emails
- ☐ Find a mailing list management hosting service
- ☐ Create an email schedule
- ☐ Be respectful of your subscribers
- ☐ Consider separate lists or segments for each artist

16. Build a Press List

- ☐ Search online for press/blog contacts
- ☐ Ask the bands on your labels for their contacts
- ☐ Ask other labels to share their contacts
- ☐ Keep a detailed spreadsheet with notes

17. Prepare Your First Release

- ☐ Pick a release date
- ☐ Choose your format(s);
    - I.   Cassette
    - II. Vinyl
    - III. CD
    - IV. Digital
- ☐ Create a workback schedule for each format

18. How to Pick a Release Date

- ☐ Avoid holidays or regional/local events
- ☐ What season matches the music best?
- ☐ What time of year is best for the artist?
    - I.   When the masters will be ready
    - II. When are they available to tour, give interviews?
    - III. When is the best time for media availability?

19. Create a Workback Schedule

- ☐ Work backwards from your release date
- ☐ Identify mile-markers that need to be reached by certain dates
- ☐ Share this with the artists and print off a copy for yourself
- ☐ How long do you need from when you receive the masters to when the record is released?

20. Choose Your Format
- [ ] Digital
  - I. Digital Service Providers (Spotify, Apple Music, iTunes, Tidal)
  - II. Bandcamp
- [ ] Physical
  - I. Cassette
  - II. Vinyl
  - III. CD
- [ ] Consider what format(s) you want your label to be known for

21. What Does it Mean to "Exploit the Masters?"
- [ ] Find unique ways to monetize the music
  - I. Licensing for film/TV/commercials
  - II. Instrumental Versions
  - III. Promote on Podcasts/Samplers
  - IV. Create alternative versions and remixes for future releases

22. Create an Album Artwork Campaign
- [ ] Give the release its own branding
- [ ] Carry that through to all promotional items
  - I. Web Banners
  - II. Social Media Banners
  - III. Album Singles
  - IV. Physical Media
  - V. Merchandise

23. Ask for Advice
- [ ] Talk to your suppliers and tell them you are new, seeking advice:
  - I. Vinyl Manufacturers
  - II. Digital Distributors
- [ ] Talk to your local record store
- [ ] Email other record labels
- [ ] Read articles, listen to podcasts, read books on record labels

24. Make a Marketing Checklist
- [ ] Create a list of promo tasks that need to be done prior to release day
  - I. Pitch lead single to playlisters
  - II. Email your press list
  - III. eBlast your fan email list
  - IV. Social media posts, stories
  - V. Bring copies to your local record store

25. Outside the Box Marketing Strategies
- ☐ Send postcards
- ☐ Pitch to third-party playlists
- ☐ Post an audio commentary on Bandcamp
- ☐ Record a track-by-track podcast
- ☐ Have other artists on your label promote the new release
- ☐ Release on Bandcamp a few days early
- ☐ Ask friends to post on social media

26. How to Get your Music on Spotify and AppleMusic
- ☐ Pick a digital distributor
  - I. CD Baby, Tunecore, DistroKid
- ☐ Give yourself proper lead time
- ☐ Upload the album to Bandcamp
- ☐ Consider only using Bandcamp

27. Make a Promo One-Sheet for Your Release
- ☐ To include;
  - I. Photo, Brief Bio, Tracklist, Barcode/Catalog ID, Contact Info, Accolades, Artist's social media, album download link
- ☐ Digital PDF
- ☐ Create a printed version if necessary

28. Encourage your Artists to be Prolific
- ☐ Release original demos
- ☐ Record acoustic versions
- ☐ Record live versions
- ☐ Special Spotify release or Bandcamp exclusive

29. Submitting Singles to Playlists
- ☐ Spotify editorial submission form (Spotify for Artists)
- ☐ Use SubmitHub or other submission portals
- ☐ Ask your friends to add the single(s) to their personal playlists
- ☐ Contact third-party curators via email or social media

30. Keep an Album alive after Release Day
- ☐ Music Video(s)
- ☐ Touring and live events
- ☐ B-Side singles, remixes
- ☐ Follow-up EP a few months later
- ☐ Expect the album to disappear from the radar immediately, so plan a follow up strategy at the same time that you are planning the pre-release strategy.
- ☐ Celebrate the album's one month and one-year anniversary

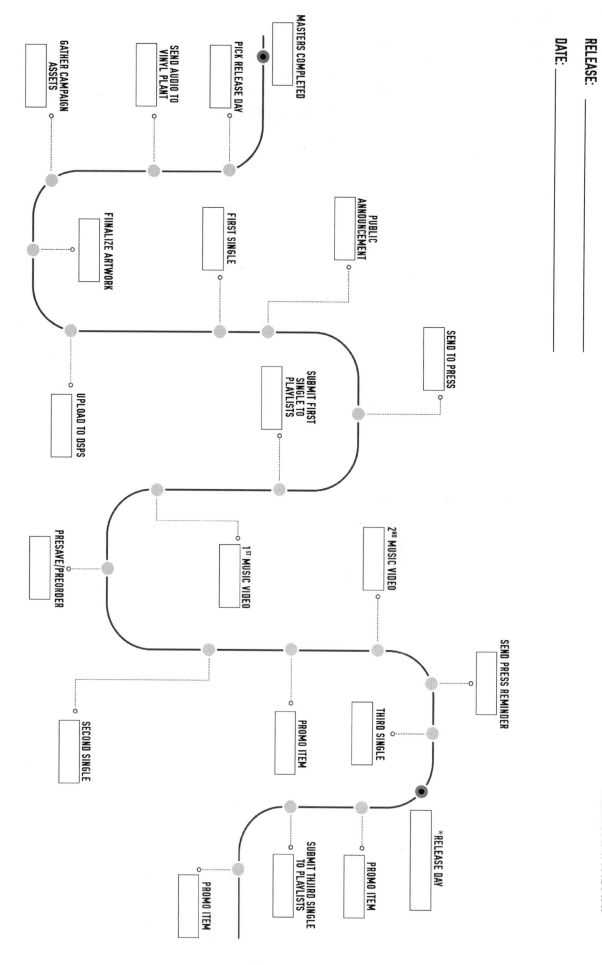

ARTIST: _____

RELEASE: _____

DATE: _____

RELEASE ROADMAP

MASTERS COMPLETED

PICK RELEASE DAY

SEND AUDIO TO VINYL PLANT

GATHER CAMPAIGN ASSETS

FIINALIZE ARTWORK

FIRST SINGLE

PUBLIC ANNOUNCEMENT

UPLOAD TO DSPS

SUBMIT FIRST SINGLE TO PLAYLISTS

SEND TO PRESS

PRESAVE/PREORDER

1ST MUSIC VIDEO

2ND MUSIC VIDEO

SECOND SINGLE

PROMO ITEM

THIRD SINGLE

SEND PRESS REMINDER

PROMO ITEM

SUBMIT THIRD SINGLE TO PLAYLISTS

PROMO ITEM

*RELEASE DAY

ARTIST:

RELEASE:

DATE:

RELEASE ROADMAP

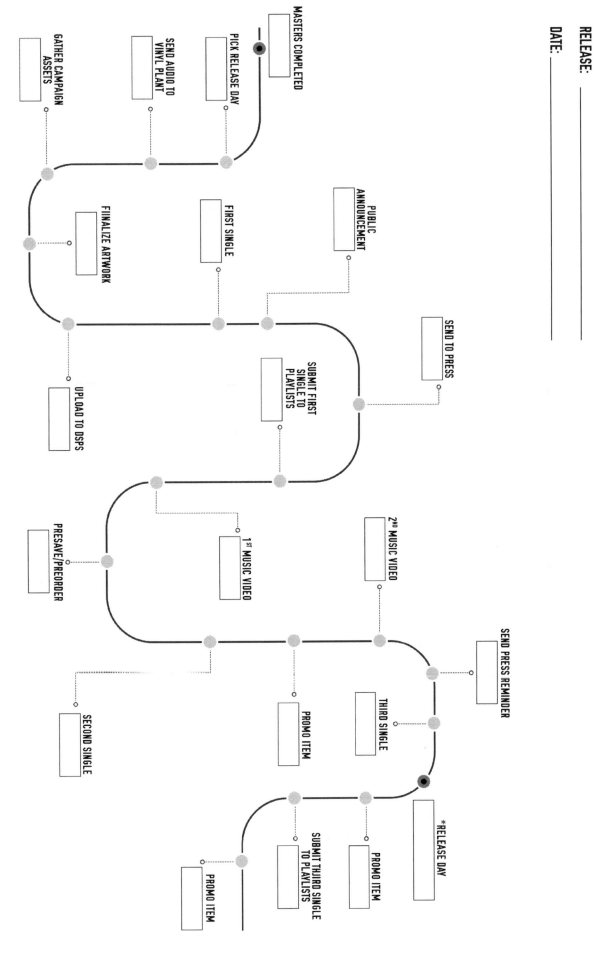

MASTERS COMPLETED

PICK RELEASE DAY

SEND AUDIO TO VINYL PLANT

GATHER CAMPAIGN ASSETS

FINALIZE ARTWORK

FIRST SINGLE

PUBLIC ANNOUNCEMENT

UPLOAD TO DSPS

SUBMIT FIRST SINGLE TO PLAYLISTS

SEND TO PRESS

PRESAVE/PREORDER

1ST MUSIC VIDEO

2ND MUSIC VIDEO

SEND PRESS REMINDER

SECOND SINGLE

PROMO ITEM

THIRD SINGLE

PROMO ITEM

SUBMIT THIRD SINGLE TO PLAYLISTS

PROMO ITEM

*RELEASE DAY

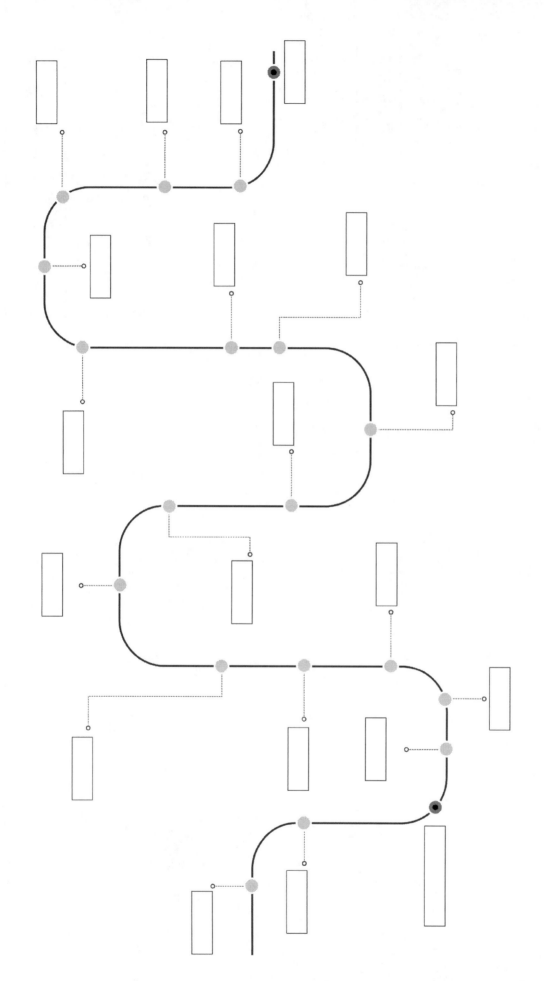

ARTIST: _____

RELEASE: _____

DATE: _____

RELEASE ROADMAP

90

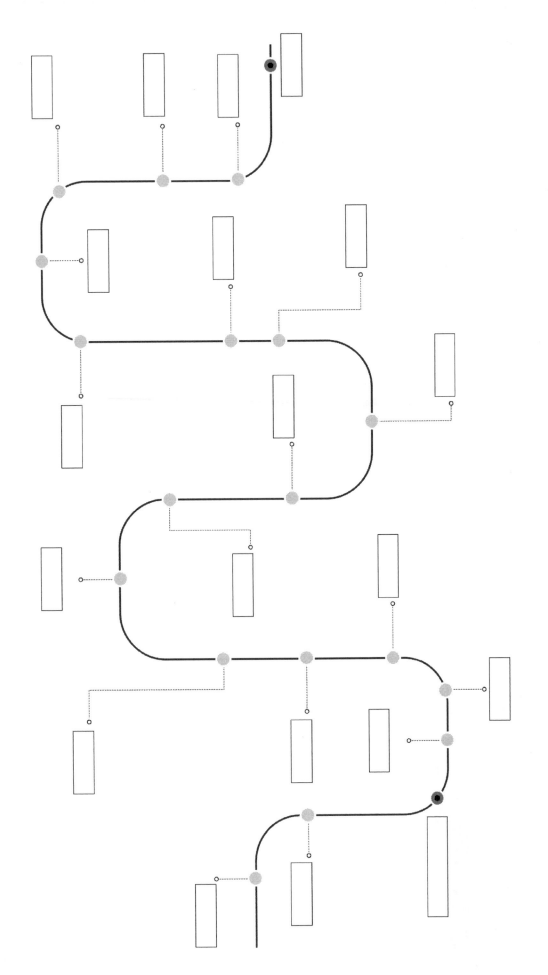

RELEASE ROADMAP

GET THE BONUS CONTENT

Visit **www.otherrecordlabels.com/workbook** for printable pages of this workbook, plus more resources to help jumpstart your new record label.

Be sure to join our private community of record labels at
http://facebook.otherrecordlabels.com

Get more weekly advice on running a record label at
https://www.otherrecordlabels.com/quick-tips

SQUARESPACE DISCOUNT

OTHERRECORDLABELS.COM/SQUARESPACE

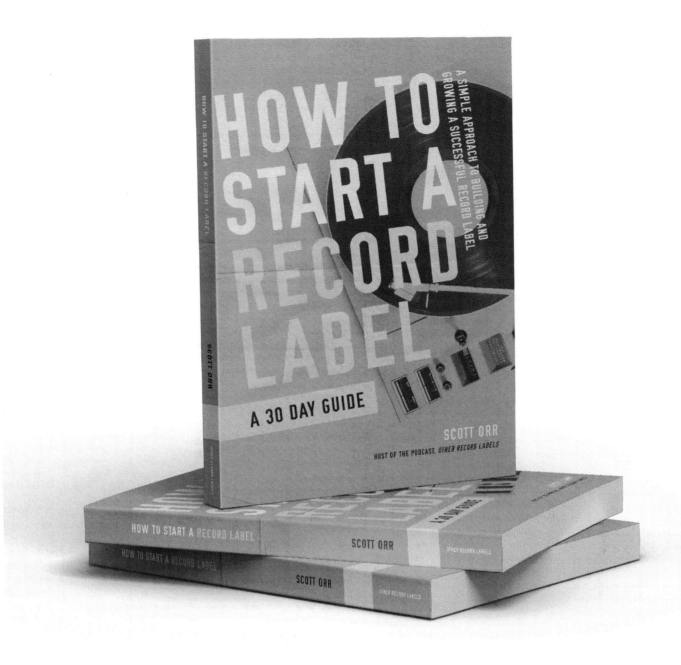

HOW TO START A RECORD LABEL: A 30 DAY GUIDE

A Simplified Approach to Building and Growing a Successful Record Label

AVAILABLE NOW ON AMAZON

otherrecordlabels.com/book

OTHERRECORDLABELS.COM

Made in the USA
Las Vegas, NV
13 October 2023

79027559R00052